# FIVE MINIATURE PRELUDES & FUGUES

## for Piano

by

# Alec Rowley

# CHESTER MUSIC

# MINIATURE PRELUDE

ALEC ROWLEY

# MINIATURE FUGUE

ALEC ROWLEY

① Subject  ② Answer  ③ Subject inverted  ④ Answer inverted

# II. PRELUDE

# II. FUGUE

① Subject   ② Answer   ③ Subject in Augmentation   ④ Stretti

# III. PRELUDE

# III. FUGUE

① Subject ② Answer ③ Stretti

# IV. PRELUDE

Andante

# IV. FUGUE

① Subject ② Answer ③ Stretti

# V. PRELUDE

① Ground bass

# V. FUGUE

① Subject ② Answer ③ Complete Stretti ④ Subject inverted and in Stretti

⑤ Final Entry

5/93 (15506)

Printed In England